WELCOME TO THE U.S.A.

OREGON

Written by Ann Heinrichs   Illustrated by Matt Kania
Content Adviser: Marianne Keddington-Lang,
Editor, Portland, Oregon

The Child's World

Published in the United States of America by The Child's World®
PO Box 326 • Chanhassen, MN 55317-0326
800-599-READ • www.childsworld.com

Photo Credits
Cover: Getty Images/Taxi/ Richard H. Johnston; frontispiece: Photodisc.

Interior: Faith Adams/Nyssa Public Library: 34; AP/Wide World Photo: 18 (Rick Bowmer), 25 (Don Ryan); Corbis: 9 (Jan Butchofsky-Houser), 10 (James Marshall), 13 (Josef Scaylea), 17 (Lowell Georgia); Philip James Corwin/Corbis: 21, 26; Mark Dunaway/University of Oregon: 29; Getty Images/Hulton|Archive/MPI: 16; National Park Service: 33; Pendleton Woolen Mills: 14; Photodisc: 6, 38; Portland Chinese Classical Garden: 22; Tillamook County Creamery Association: 30.

Acknowledgments
The Child's World®: Mary Berendes, Publishing Director

Editorial Directions, Inc.: E. Russell Primm, Editorial Director; Katie Marsico, Associate Editor; Judith Shiffer, Assistant Editor; Matt Messbarger, Editorial Assistant; Susan Hindman, Copy Editor; Melissa McDaniel, Proofreader; Kevin Cunningham, Peter Garnham, Matt Messbarger, Olivia Nellums, Chris Simms, Molly Symmonds, Katherine Trickle, Carl Stephen Wender, Fact Checkers; Tim Griffin/IndexServ, Indexer; Cian Loughlin O'Day, Photo Researcher and Editor

The Design Lab: Kathleen Petelinsek, Design; Julia Goozen, Art Production

Library of Congress Cataloging-in-Publication Data
Heinrichs, Ann.
  Oregon / by Ann Heinrichs : cartography and illustrations by Matt Kania.
    p. cm. — (Welcome to the U.S.A.)
  Includes index.
  ISBN 1-59296-479-6 (library bound : alk. paper) 1. Oregon—Juvenile literature.
I. Kania, Matt, ill. II. Title.
  F876.3.H45 2006
  979.5—dc22   2005009890

Ann Heinrichs is the author of more than 100 books for children and young adults. She has also enjoyed successful careers as a children's book editor and an advertising copywriter. Ann grew up in Fort Smith, Arkansas, and lives in Chicago, Illinois.

**About the Author
Ann Heinrichs**

Matt Kania loves maps and, as a kid, dreamed of making them. In school he studied geography and cartography, and today he makes maps for a living. Matt's favorite thing about drawing maps is learning about the places they represent. Many of the maps he has created can be found in books, magazines, videos, Web sites, and public places.

**About the
Map Illustrator
Matt Kania**

On the cover: **Visit Crown Point! You'll get a beautiful view of Oregon's Columbia River Gorge.**
On page one: **The citizens of Portland sleep under a starry sky.**

OUR OREGON TRIP

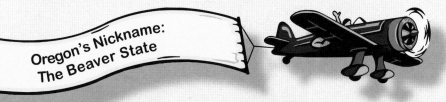

Hey! Are you up for a trip through Oregon? You'll have so many adventures there!

You'll raft down a rushing river. You'll swim in a volcano. You'll hunt for **fossils** and sparkly rocks. You'll see how cheese and blankets are made. You'll meet sea lions and wild horses. You'll gaze at distant stars. And you'll watch salmon leap uphill!

Are you ready? Then let's not wait. Just buckle up and hang on tight. We're off to see Oregon!

WELCOME TO OREGON

As you travel through Oregon, watch for all the interesting facts along the way.

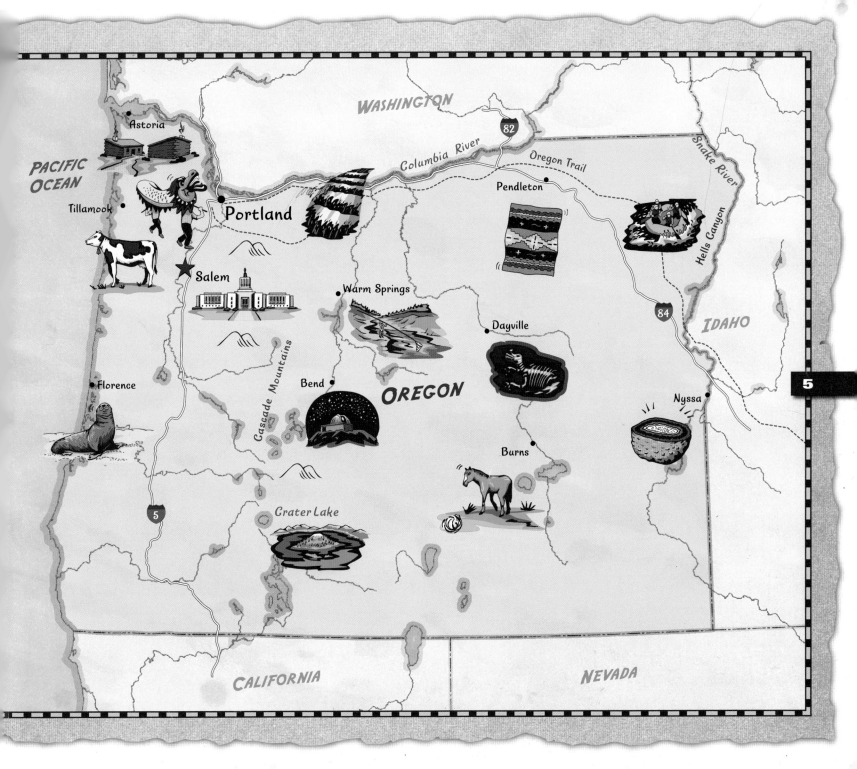

PACIFIC OCEAN

WASHINGTON

Astoria

Tillamook

Portland

Columbia River

Oregon Trail

Pendleton

Snake River

Hells Canyon

IDAHO

Salem

Warm Springs

Dayville

OREGON

Florence

Cascade Mountains

Bend

Nyssa

Burns

Crater Lake

CALIFORNIA

NEVADA

82

84

5

Mount Mazama erupted and then collapsed. That created Crater Lake.

Can you believe this was once a huge volcano? It looks pretty peaceful now.

The High Desert Museum is in Bend. It explores the history, wildlife, and landscape of central and eastern Oregon's desert regions.

Oregon Caves National Monument is near Cave Junction. Visitors love the caves' spectacular rock formations.

Crater Lake in the Cascade Mountains

Want to swim in a volcano? Then jump into Crater Lake. It's a volcanic crater called a caldera!

Crater Lake is in the Cascade Mountains. These snowcapped peaks are Oregon's biggest mountain range. They tower over meadows, forests, and swift streams.

The Columbia River flows through the Cascades. Finally, it flows into the Pacific Ocean. Oregon's western border faces the ocean.

The Willamette River valley runs through western Oregon. It's known for its fertile farmland. Central and eastern Oregon are rocky and dry. The Snake River runs along the eastern border. It carves out a deep gorge called Hells Canyon.

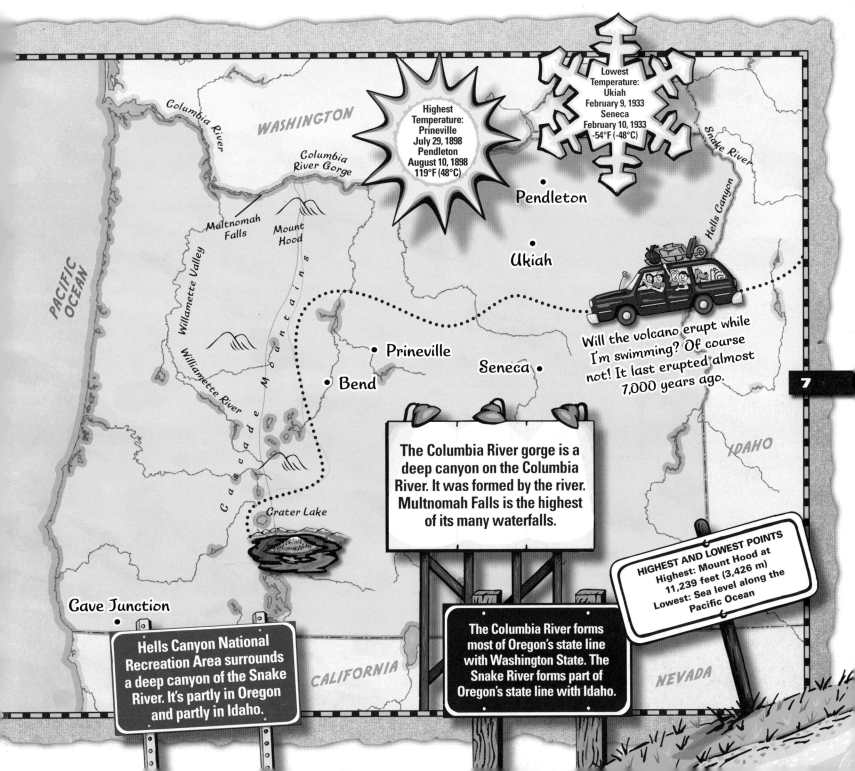

Highest
Temperature:
Prineville
July 29, 1898
Pendleton
August 10, 1898
119°F (48°C)

Lowest
Temperature:
Ukiah
February 9, 1933
Seneca
February 10, 1933
-54°F (-48°C)

WASHINGTON

Columbia River

Columbia
River Gorge

Multnomah
Falls

Mount
Hood

Willamette Valley

Willamette River

PACIFIC
OCEAN

Cascade Mountains

Crater Lake

Cave Junction

Pendleton

Ukiah

Prineville

Bend

Seneca

Snake River

Hells Canyon

IDAHO

CALIFORNIA

NEVADA

Will the volcano erupt while
I'm swimming? Of course
not! It last erupted almost
7,000 years ago.

The Columbia River gorge is a
deep canyon on the Columbia
River. It was formed by the river.
Multnomah Falls is the highest
of its many waterfalls.

HIGHEST AND LOWEST POINTS
Highest: Mount Hood at
11,239 feet (3,426 m)
Lowest: Sea level along the
Pacific Ocean

Hells Canyon National
Recreation Area surrounds
a deep canyon of the Snake
River. It's partly in Oregon
and partly in Idaho.

The Columbia River forms
most of Oregon's state line
with Washington State. The
Snake River forms part of
Oregon's state line with Idaho.

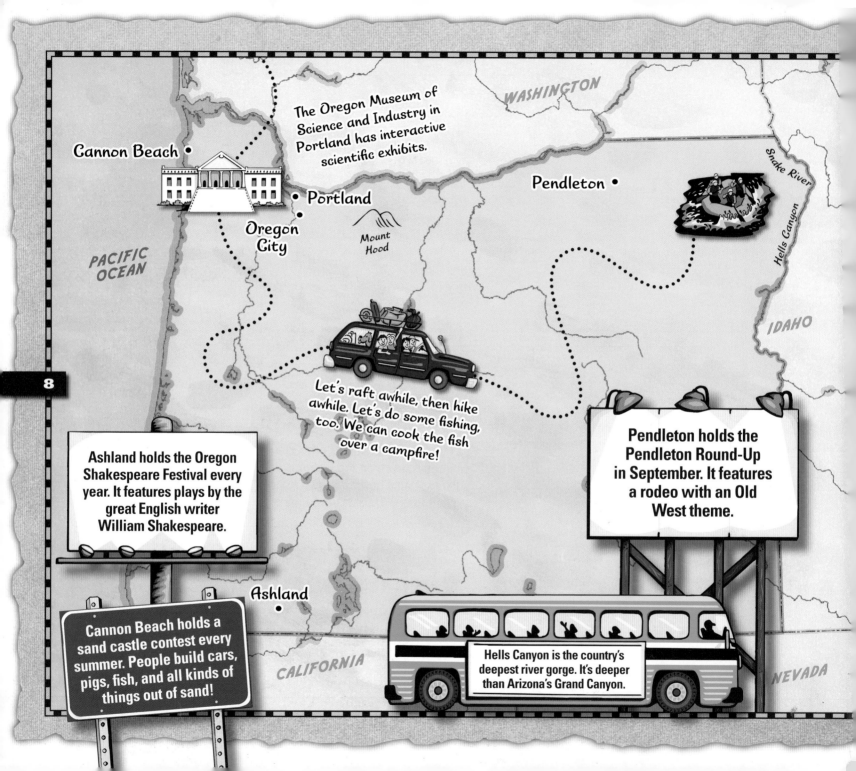

The Oregon Museum of Science and Industry in Portland has interactive scientific exhibits.

Cannon Beach •

WASHINGTON

Pendleton •

Snake River

Portland •

Oregon City •

Mount Hood

Hells Canyon

PACIFIC OCEAN

IDAHO

Let's raft awhile, then hike awhile. Let's do some fishing, too. We can cook the fish over a campfire!

Ashland holds the Oregon Shakespeare Festival every year. It features plays by the great English writer William Shakespeare.

Pendleton holds the Pendleton Round-Up in September. It features a rodeo with an Old West theme.

Ashland •

Cannon Beach holds a sand castle contest every summer. People build cars, pigs, fish, and all kinds of things out of sand!

CALIFORNIA

Hells Canyon is the country's deepest river gorge. It's deeper than Arizona's Grand Canyon.

NEVADA

Fun at Hells Canyon

Matt Groening invented The Simpsons cartoons. He was born in Portland.

Yahoo! You're bouncing past big rocks. And water's spraying all over you. You're rafting through Hells Canyon!

People love this area along the Snake River. They can hike or ride horses there, too.

Snowcapped Mount Hood is another favorite spot. Many cities hold winter carnivals and skiing contests. Rodeos are popular events, too.

You'll see sand dunes and rocky cliffs along the coast. Exploring the mountains is fun, too.

The trip through Hells Canyon is beautiful. Just be sure to hang on tight!

Oregon's 1st library opened in Oregon City in 1834. It was a subscription library and open to everyone.

Herds of pronghorn antelope live in Hart Mountain National Antelope Refuge near Plush.

These caves look creepy, but sea lions love them. Can you hear them barking?

10

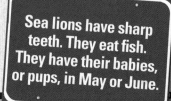

Sea lions have sharp teeth. They eat fish. They have their babies, or pups, in May or June.

Sea Lion Caves near Florence

Head down to the rocky coast. Soon you'll hear a terrible racket. Is it barking dogs? Or roaring lions? Neither. It's sea lions!

You're visiting Sea Lion Caves. About 200 sea lions live there. Some hang out in the cave. Others lounge on the rocks. And they all make lots of noise!

You'll spot many other animals along the coast. Sometimes giant whales are swimming offshore. People come from miles around to see them.

Deer, elk, and bighorn sheep live in the mountains. East of the Cascades, you'll find antelope. Almost half the state is forestland. Foxes, coyotes, and beavers make their homes there.

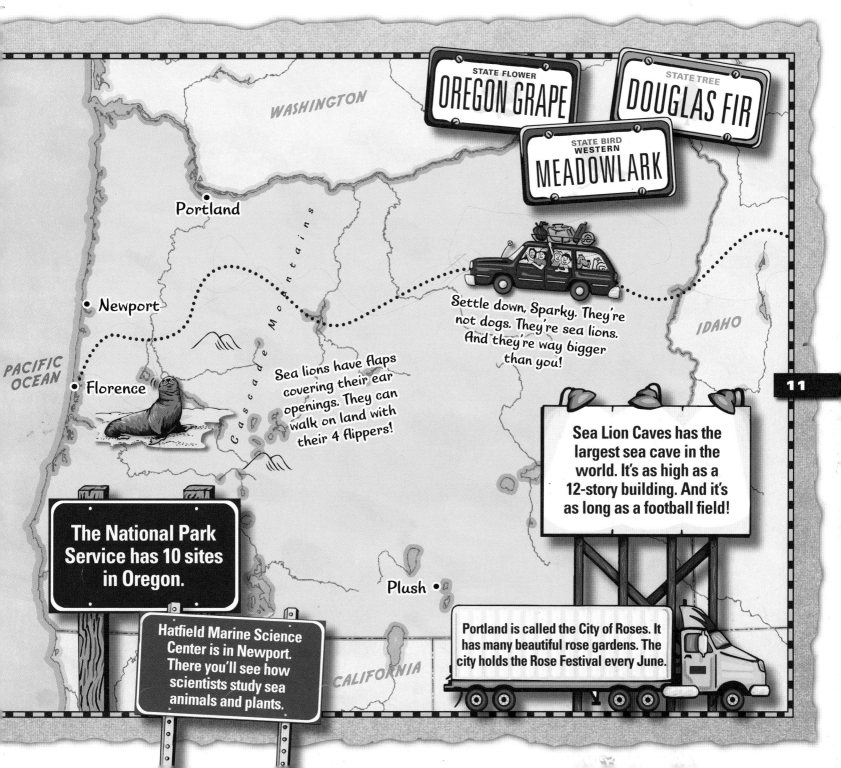

STATE FLOWER
OREGON GRAPE

STATE TREE
DOUGLAS FIR

STATE BIRD
WESTERN
MEADOWLARK

Settle down, Sparky. They're not dogs. They're sea lions. And they're way bigger than you!

Sea lions have flaps covering their ear openings. They can walk on land with their 4 flippers!

Sea Lion Caves has the largest sea cave in the world. It's as high as a 12-story building. And it's as long as a football field!

The National Park Service has 10 sites in Oregon.

Hatfield Marine Science Center is in Newport. There you'll see how scientists study sea animals and plants.

Portland is called the City of Roses. It has many beautiful rose gardens. The city holds the Rose Festival every June.

WASHINGTON

Portland

Newport

PACIFIC OCEAN

Florence

Cascade Mountains

IDAHO

Plush

CALIFORNIA

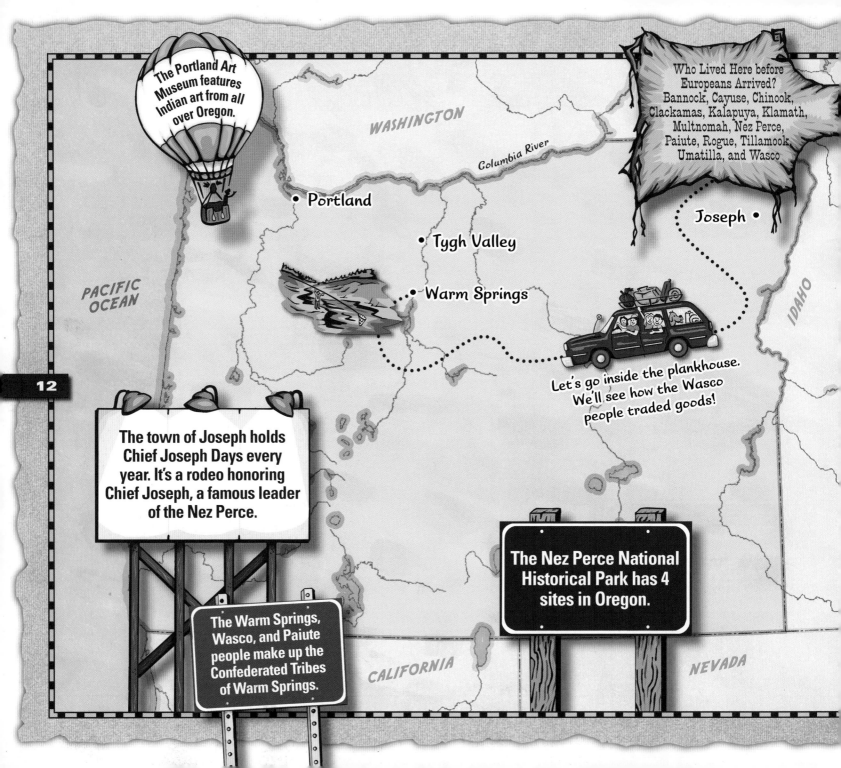

The Portland Art Museum features Indian art from all over Oregon.

Who Lived Here before Europeans Arrived? Bannock, Cayuse, Chinook, Clackamas, Kalapuya, Klamath, Multnomah, Nez Perce, Paiute, Rogue, Tillamook, Umatilla, and Wasco

WASHINGTON

Columbia River

• Portland

• Tygh Valley

• Warm Springs

PACIFIC OCEAN

Joseph •

IDAHO

Let's go inside the plankhouse. We'll see how the Wasco people traded goods!

The town of Joseph holds Chief Joseph Days every year. It's a rodeo honoring Chief Joseph, a famous leader of the Nez Perce.

The Nez Perce National Historical Park has 4 sites in Oregon.

The Warm Springs, Wasco, and Paiute people make up the Confederated Tribes of Warm Springs.

CALIFORNIA

NEVADA

The Museum at Warm Springs

Step inside a Native American **plankhouse.** See Indian masks, tools, baskets, and clothes. Hear tribal **elders** tell **traditional** tales. You're visiting the Museum at Warm Springs! It's on the Warm Springs **Reservation.** Three Indian groups live here. They were moved here from their homelands in 1885.

These people found plentiful food in the forest. They dug for roots with special digging sticks. Deer and other large animals provided meat. Other Indians lived along the Columbia River. They caught salmon with long spears. They dried and stored the fish for winter.

Visitors to Warm Springs can view Native American artifacts. This decorative headdress is especially impressive.

The All-Indian Rodeo is held in Tygh Valley every year.

Watch the looms weave. This colorful fabric will make a great blanket.

Indian Blankets at Pendleton Woolen Mills

Here come big bundles of brightly colored wool. Spinning machines spin it into yarn. Then the yarn goes to the weaving room. The noisy looms weave it into rugs!

You're touring Pendleton Woolen Mills. It makes blankets that have traditional Indian designs.

Oregon's factories make all kinds of goods. Electronic equipment is the top factory product. That includes computer parts and calculators. Wood products are important, too. Forest trees are made into lumber, cardboard, and paper.

You can tour Rodgers Instruments in Hillsboro. It makes pipe organs and electronic organs.

Pacific Hazelnut Candy Factory is in Aurora.

WASHINGTON

• Hillsboro

• Aurora

Pendleton •

Blue Mountains

PACIFIC OCEAN

IDAHO

What's that pounding noise? It seems like the walls are shaking! Oh, it's just those monster weaving machines.

What's Made in Oregon? Electrical equipment, wood products, metals, and food products

Many Indians shop at Pendleton Woolen Mills. They buy blankets for themselves or to give as gifts on important occasions.

What's Mined in Oregon? Sand and gravel, crushed stone, cement, diatomite, lime, and pumice

CALIFORNIA

More than 2,000 sheep graze in the Blue Mountains near Pendleton. Their wool becomes Pendleton blankets.

NEVADA

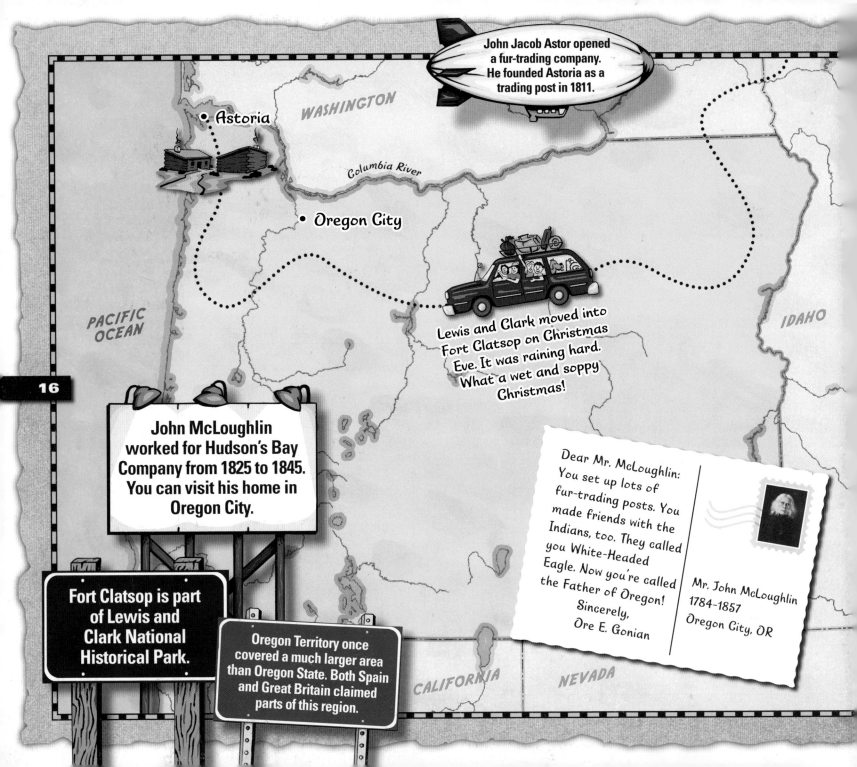

John Jacob Astor opened a fur-trading company. He founded Astoria as a trading post in 1811.

WASHINGTON

• Astoria

Columbia River

• Oregon City

PACIFIC OCEAN

IDAHO

Lewis and Clark moved into Fort Clatsop on Christmas Eve. It was raining hard. What a wet and soppy Christmas!

16

John McLoughlin worked for Hudson's Bay Company from 1825 to 1845. You can visit his home in Oregon City.

Dear Mr. McLoughlin:
You set up lots of fur-trading posts. You made friends with the Indians, too. They called you White-Headed Eagle. Now you're called the Father of Oregon!
Sincerely,
Ore E. Gonian

Mr. John McLoughlin
1784-1857
Oregon City, OR

Fort Clatsop is part of Lewis and Clark National Historical Park.

Oregon Territory once covered a much larger area than Oregon State. Both Spain and Great Britain claimed parts of this region.

CALIFORNIA   NEVADA

Fort Clatsop near Astoria

Timber! People carve logs into dugout canoes at Fort Clatsop.

Some people are carving logs into canoes. Others are making candles or smoking meat. Everyone's dressed like people from the 1800s. It's a living-history program at Fort Clatsop!

Explorers camped here during the winter of 1805–1806. They were led by Meriwether Lewis and William Clark. These men had come west from Missouri. They hoped to reach the Pacific Ocean. And they did! They followed the Columbia River to the ocean.

Fur traders soon arrived in Oregon. They set up many trading posts. Missionaries settled in Oregon in 1834. Soon a flood of settlers poured in!

Lewis and Clark named Fort Clatsop after the local Clatsop Indians.

The End of the Oregon Trail Interpretive Center

Check out the big covered wagons. Watch the **pioneers** work and cook. Walk along deep **ruts** in the ground. The wheels from real pioneers' wagons dug those ruts! You're visiting the End of the Oregon Trail Interpretive Center. It's in Oregon City. It explores life along the Oregon Trail.

Thousands of people headed west along that trail. They traveled it from the 1840s to the 1880s. They had heard about the Willamette Valley. They hoped to begin farming there.

Indians and settlers sometimes clashed. The Indians were being pushed off their homelands. Finally, they were forced onto reservations.

This wagon has wooden wheels. Imagine what a bumpy ride pioneers had!

The Oregon Trail was rough. It crossed mountains, rivers, and deserts. The trip across the entire trail took about 6 months.

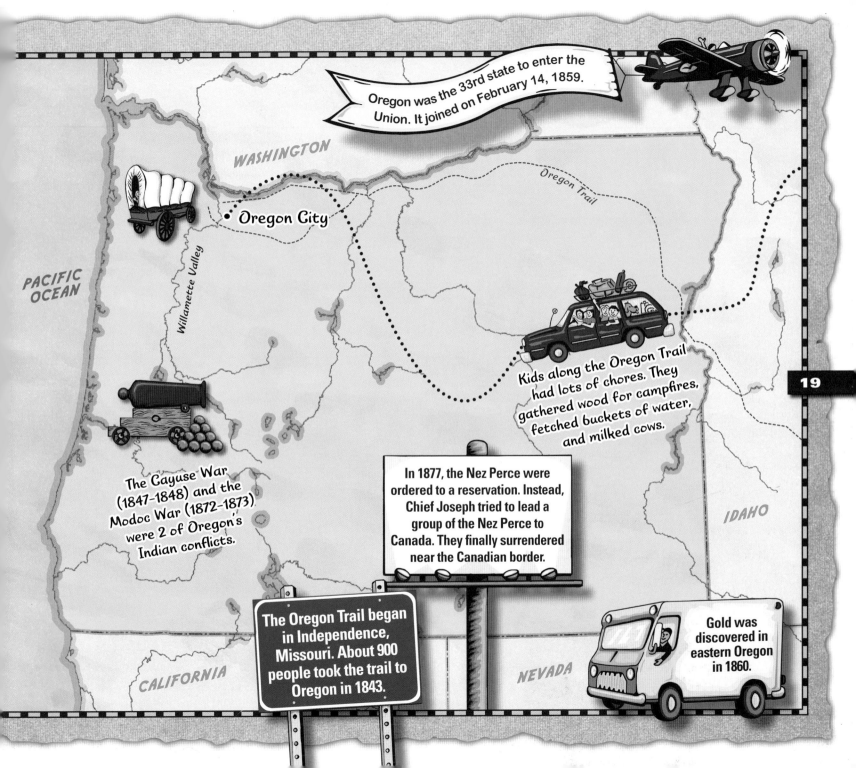

Oregon was the 33rd state to enter the Union. It joined on February 14, 1859.

WASHINGTON

Oregon Trail

Oregon City

PACIFIC OCEAN

Willamette Valley

Kids along the Oregon Trail had lots of chores. They gathered wood for campfires, fetched buckets of water, and milked cows.

The Cayuse War (1847–1848) and the Modoc War (1872–1873) were 2 of Oregon's Indian conflicts.

In 1877, the Nez Perce were ordered to a reservation. Instead, Chief Joseph tried to lead a group of the Nez Perce to Canada. They finally surrendered near the Canadian border.

IDAHO

The Oregon Trail began in Independence, Missouri. About 900 people took the trail to Oregon in 1843.

CALIFORNIA

NEVADA

Gold was discovered in eastern Oregon in 1860.

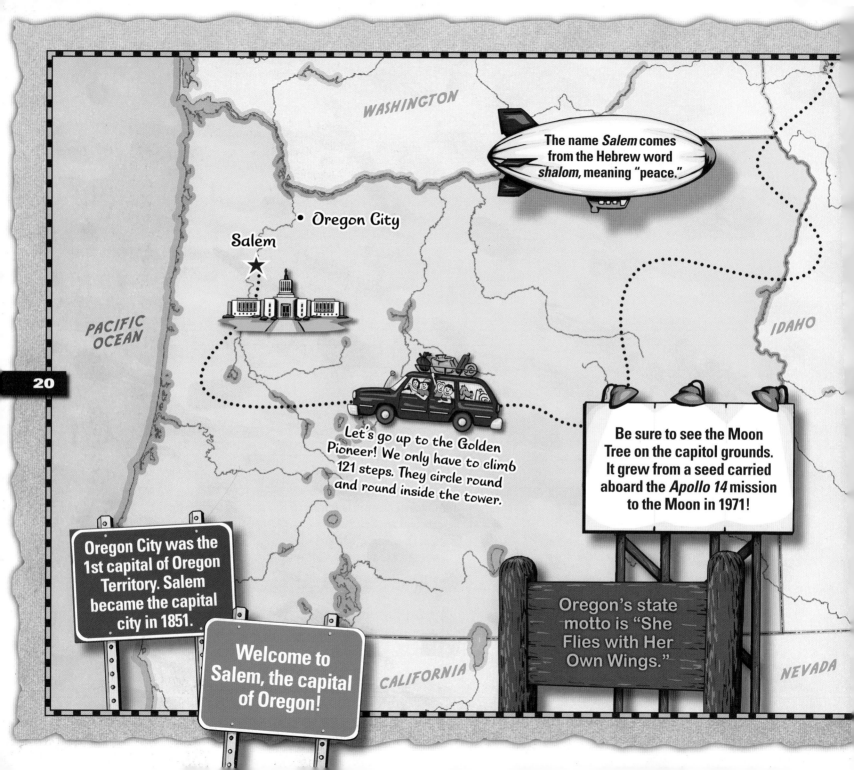

The name *Salem* comes from the Hebrew word *shalom*, meaning "peace."

• Oregon City

Salem

PACIFIC OCEAN

WASHINGTON

IDAHO

20

Let's go up to the Golden Pioneer! We only have to climb 121 steps. They circle round and round inside the tower.

Be sure to see the Moon Tree on the capitol grounds. It grew from a seed carried aboard the *Apollo 14* mission to the Moon in 1971!

Oregon City was the 1st capital of Oregon Territory. Salem became the capital city in 1851.

Welcome to Salem, the capital of Oregon!

Oregon's state motto is "She Flies with Her Own Wings."

CALIFORNIA

NEVADA

The State Capitol in Salem

See that statue atop the capitol? It glistens in the sunlight. It's the Golden Pioneer! This statue honors Oregon's early settlers. They had to be tough to survive! Then step inside the capitol. You'll see huge paintings of pioneer life.

The capitol is the center of state government. Oregon's government has three branches. The Legislative Assembly makes up one branch. Its members make the state's laws. You can even watch them at work. The governor leads another branch. This branch carries out the laws. The third branch applies the law to court cases. This branch is made up of judges.

Check out the beautiful statue atop the capitol! It reminds people of Oregon's brave pioneers.

You can visit Mission Mill Village in Salem. It has historic houses and working mill equipment. Mills were early factories.

Watch out for the dragon! People celebrate Chinese New Year in Portland.

Chinese New Year in Portland

Snap, crackle, pop! Fireworks are exploding everywhere. And a giant dragon snakes down the street. It's Chinese New Year in Portland!

Thousands of Chinese **immigrants** moved to Oregon. The biggest move came in the late 1800s. Chinese people were Portland's largest ethnic group then. Today, Chinese people live all over the state. They still celebrate their special holidays.

Immigrants arrived from many other countries. Some came from Germany, England, or Ireland. Others came from Norway, Sweden, or Italy. They all made new homes in Oregon.

Portland's Chinese New Year celebration lasts 2 weeks.

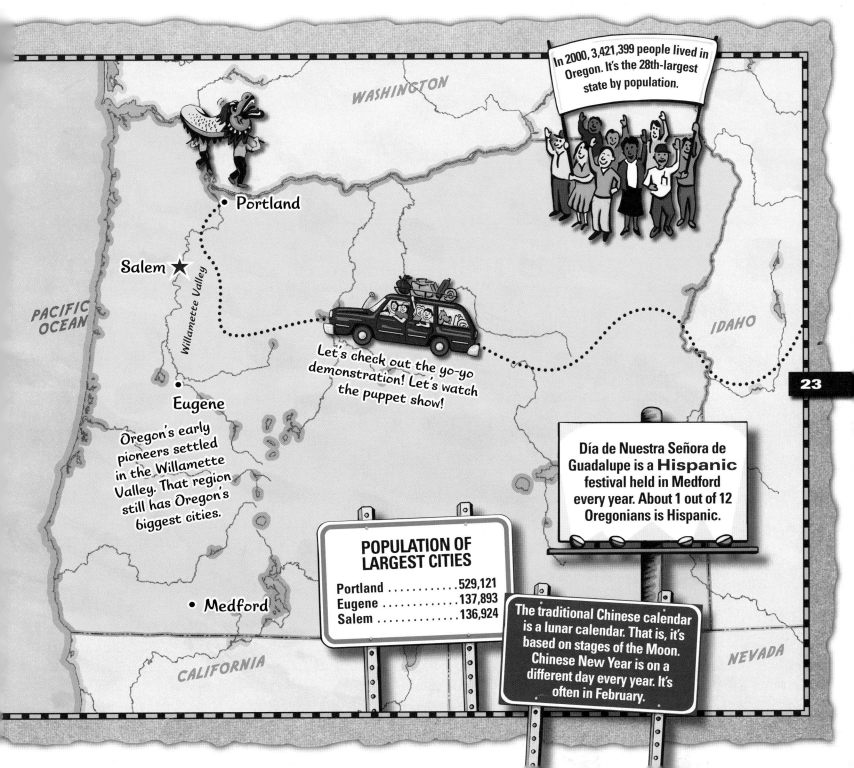

In 2000, 3,421,399 people lived in Oregon. It's the 28th-largest state by population.

WASHINGTON

Portland

Salem ★

PACIFIC OCEAN

Willamette Valley

Eugene

Oregon's early pioneers settled in the Willamette Valley. That region still has Oregon's biggest cities.

Medford

CALIFORNIA

Let's check out the yo-yo demonstration! Let's watch the puppet show!

IDAHO

Día de Nuestra Señora de Guadalupe is a **Hispanic** festival held in Medford every year. About 1 out of 12 Oregonians is Hispanic.

POPULATION OF LARGEST CITIES

Portland 529,121
Eugene 137,893
Salem 136,924

The traditional Chinese calendar is a lunar calendar. That is, it's based on stages of the Moon. Chinese New Year is on a different day every year. It's often in February.

NEVADA

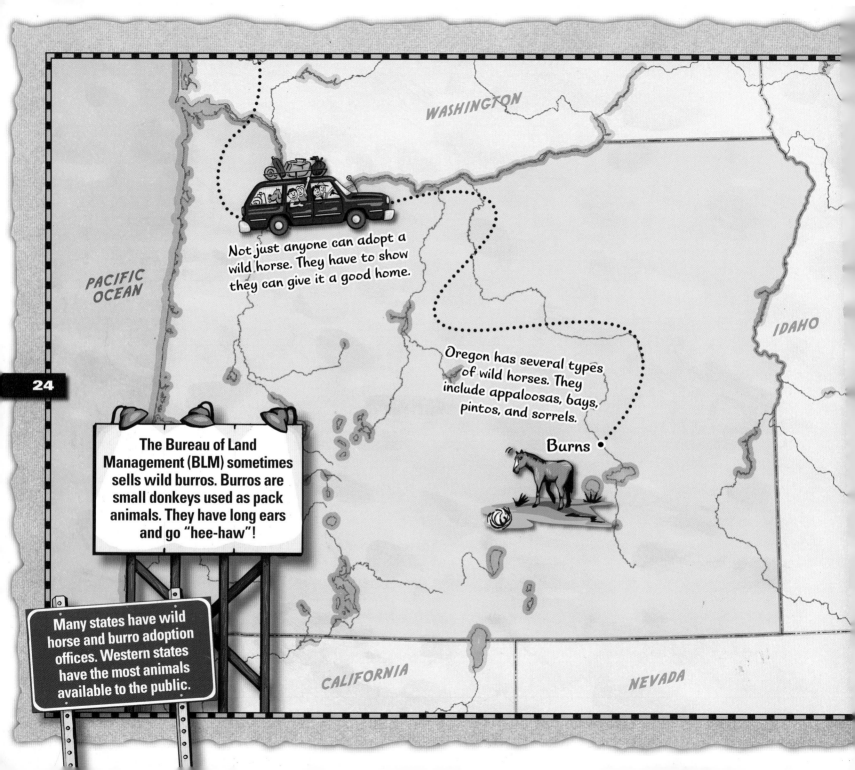

Not just anyone can adopt a wild horse. They have to show they can give it a good home.

Oregon has several types of wild horses. They include appaloosas, bays, pintos, and sorrels.

Burns

The Bureau of Land Management (BLM) sometimes sells wild burros. Burros are small donkeys used as pack animals. They have long ears and go "hee-haw"!

Many states have wild horse and burro adoption offices. Western states have the most animals available to the public.

PACIFIC OCEAN

WASHINGTON

IDAHO

CALIFORNIA

NEVADA

The Wild Horse Roundup

The BLM looks after wild horses on public lands.

Have you ever seen a wild horse? Just visit the Wild Horse **Corrals** near Burns. You'll see dozens of these beautiful animals there.

Thousands of wild horses roam around Oregon. Their **ancestors** escaped from settlers or miners. Sometimes the herds grow too big. There's not enough grass for them all. Then cowboys ride out on the range. They round up lots of horses. Helicopters help with the roundup, too.

The horses are herded into holding pens. Next they're brought to the corral. Then some people are allowed to adopt a horse. They can give it lots of space and food.

Giddyup! These wild horses are galloping around at the Wild Horse Corrals.

Have you ever seen a salmon jump?
You will at Bonneville Dam!

Oregon is on one side of Bonneville Dam. Washington State is on the other side.

Fish Ladders at Bonneville Dam

Splash, splash! You're watching salmon jump up the fish ladder. You're at Bonneville Dam! This dam is on the Columbia River near Portland. It was built to create water-powered electricity. The dam created problems for salmon, though.

Salmon are born farther up the river. Then they swim down to the ocean. In time, they're ready to reproduce. They swim back upriver to do this. But the dam is in their way. That's why fish ladders were built. The ladders are like pools arranged in stair steps. The fish jump to higher and higher levels.

Bonneville Dam opened in 1938. Oregon built many more dams. And a lot of them have fish ladders!

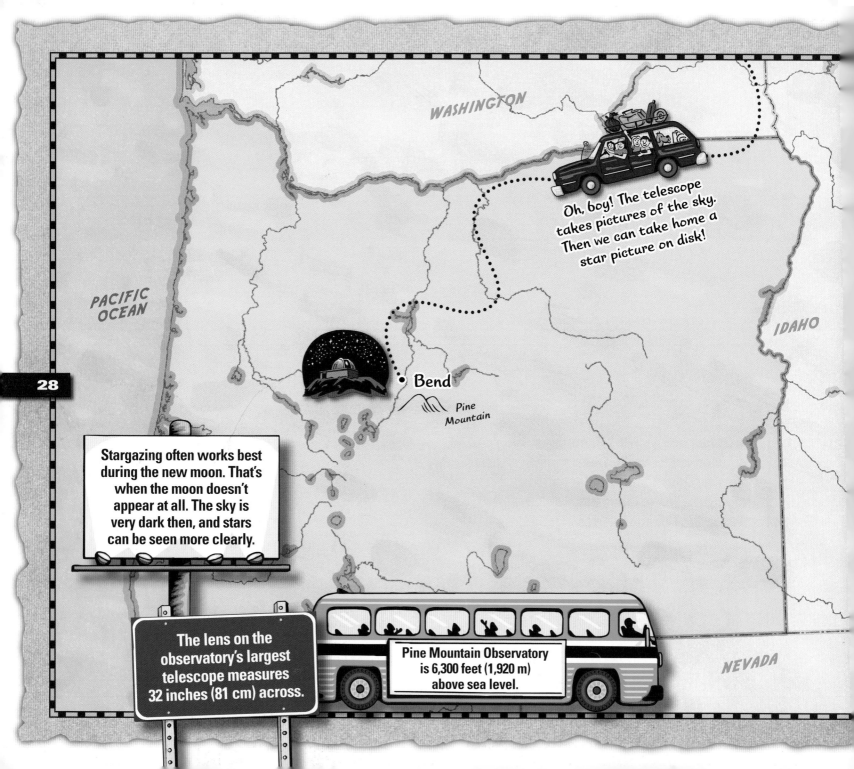

WASHINGTON

IDAHO

PACIFIC OCEAN

Oh, boy! The telescope takes pictures of the sky. Then we can take home a star picture on disk!

• Bend

Pine Mountain

NEVADA

Stargazing often works best during the new moon. That's when the moon doesn't appear at all. The sky is very dark then, and stars can be seen more clearly.

The lens on the observatory's largest telescope measures 32 inches (81 cm) across.

Pine Mountain Observatory is 6,300 feet (1,920 m) above sea level.

Stargazing on Pine Mountain

Do you like staying up late? Then visit Pine Mountain **Observatory**! This stargazing center is near Bend. It sits high atop Pine Mountain.

The observatory has three massive telescopes. They let you see objects in the night sky. Sometimes the skies are extremely clear. Then people keep watching all night!

The University of Oregon owns this observatory. Scientists study the stars there. They might see black holes or exploding stars. Their discoveries are important. They help solve the mysteries of the universe. Maybe you'll solve some mysteries, too!

Peek at the stars from Pine Mountain! Maybe you'll spot a shooting star!

People can visit Pine Mountain Observatory Friday and Saturday evenings from late May through late September.

Yum! Tour the Tillamook Cheese factory. Maybe even take some Oregon cheese home with you.

Where is Tillamook Cheese? In Tillamook! It's the center of the dairy industry along Oregon's coast.

Touring Tillamook Cheese

Do you like grilled-cheese sandwiches? That cheese started out as milk. How did it turn into cheese? Just visit Tillamook Cheese. You'll see how it all happens!

First, workers cook the milk. It separates into **curds** and **whey.** They drain off the whey. Then they press the curds into blocks. Presto! Cheese!

Milk is an important farm product in Oregon. Farmers raise both dairy and beef cattle. Greenhouse and nursery plants are the top crops. Oregon is good at growing flowers from **bulbs.**

Forest trees are leading products, too. Some of them end up as Christmas trees!

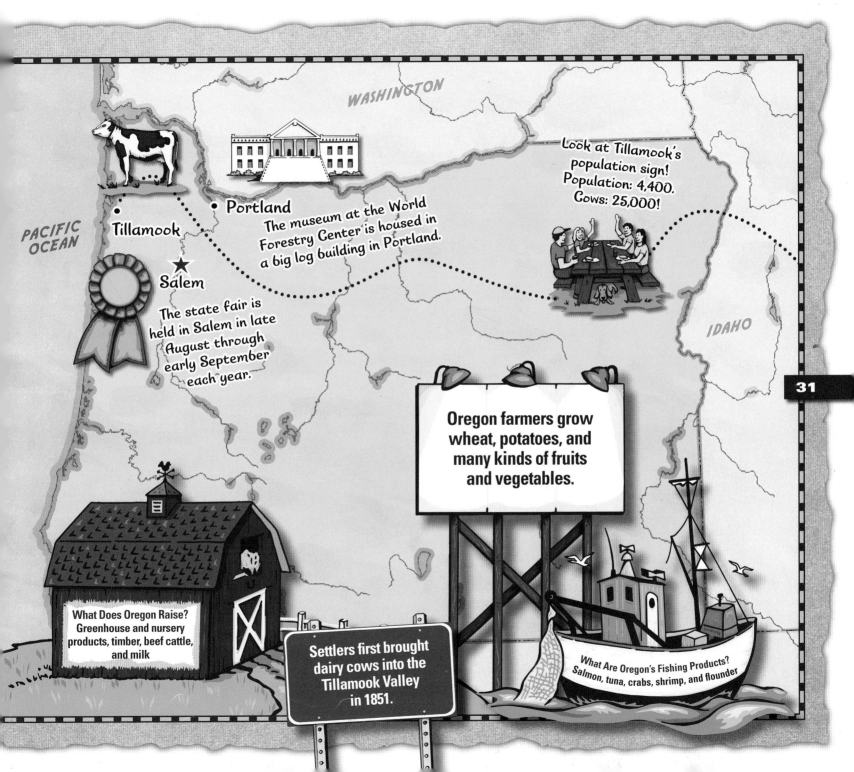

WASHINGTON

PACIFIC OCEAN

• Tillamook

• Portland

★ Salem

IDAHO

Look at Tillamook's population sign! Population: 4,400. Cows: 25,000!

The museum at the World Forestry Center is housed in a big log building in Portland.

The state fair is held in Salem in late August through early September each year.

Oregon farmers grow wheat, potatoes, and many kinds of fruits and vegetables.

What Does Oregon Raise? Greenhouse and nursery products, timber, beef cattle, and milk

Settlers first brought dairy cows into the Tillamook Valley in 1851.

What Are Oregon's Fishing Products? Salmon, tuna, crabs, shrimp, and flounder

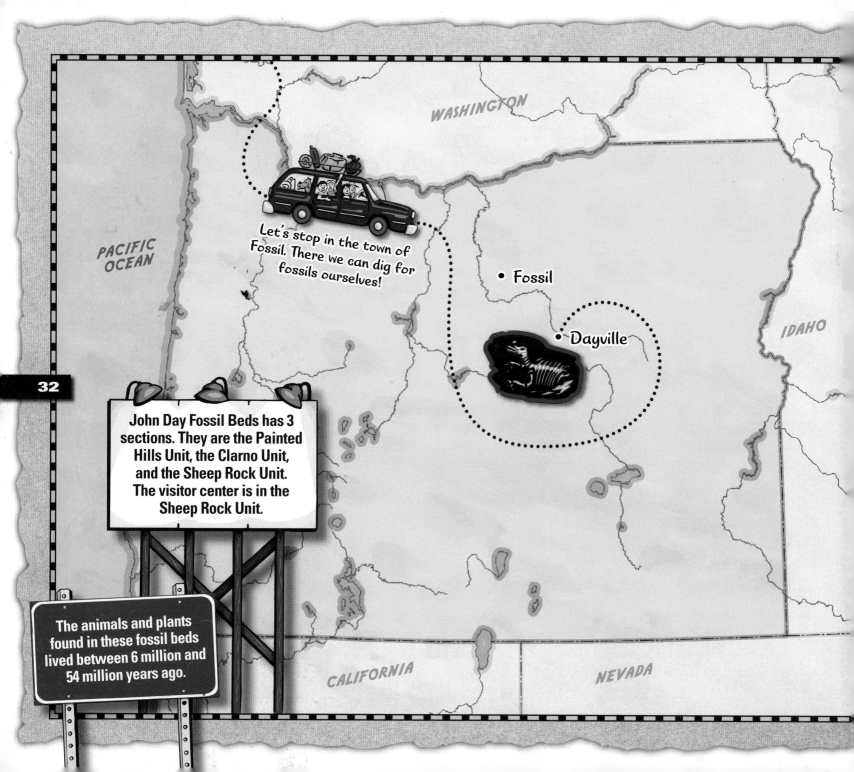

WASHINGTON

PACIFIC OCEAN

IDAHO

Let's stop in the town of Fossil. There we can dig for fossils ourselves!

• Fossil

• Dayville

John Day Fossil Beds has 3 sections. They are the Painted Hills Unit, the Clarno Unit, and the Sheep Rock Unit. The visitor center is in the Sheep Rock Unit.

The animals and plants found in these fossil beds lived between 6 million and 54 million years ago.

CALIFORNIA

NEVADA

John Day Fossil Beds

You see an enormous jawbone. Your arm could fit in that mouth! It belonged to an early rhinoceros. It was found at John Day Fossil Beds.

This site is in north-central Oregon. It spreads across a big area. You'll see that jawbone in the museum. It's in the visitor center near Dayville.

Many scientists work at the fossil beds. They dig up fossils there. Then they study them. They've found fossils of fish, birds, insects, and plants. They've found horses, saber-toothed cats, and sea tortoises. You can watch the scientists at work. Just drop by the museum!

Stop by John Day Fossil Beds! Visitors can watch scientists dig up dinosaur bones!

You'll see petrified wood in the fossil bed area. That's wood that has turned to stone over millions of years.

Thundereggs at Succor Creek

Whoa! I wouldn't try frying this egg! Check out the thunderegg collection at Succor Creek.

Nyssa holds a rock show called Thunderegg Days every year.

You've heard of thunderclouds. You've heard of thunderstorms. Maybe you've even heard of thunderbirds. But have you ever heard of thundereggs?

The thunderegg is Oregon's state rock. Thundereggs don't look that great on the outside. They're just sort of lumpy and brown. But crack a thunderegg open. The inside sparkles like colored glass!

You can hunt for thundereggs at many sites. Succor Creek State National Area near Nyssa is a good spot. Some thundereggs are as small as marbles. But others can weigh hundreds of pounds. Happy rock-hunting!

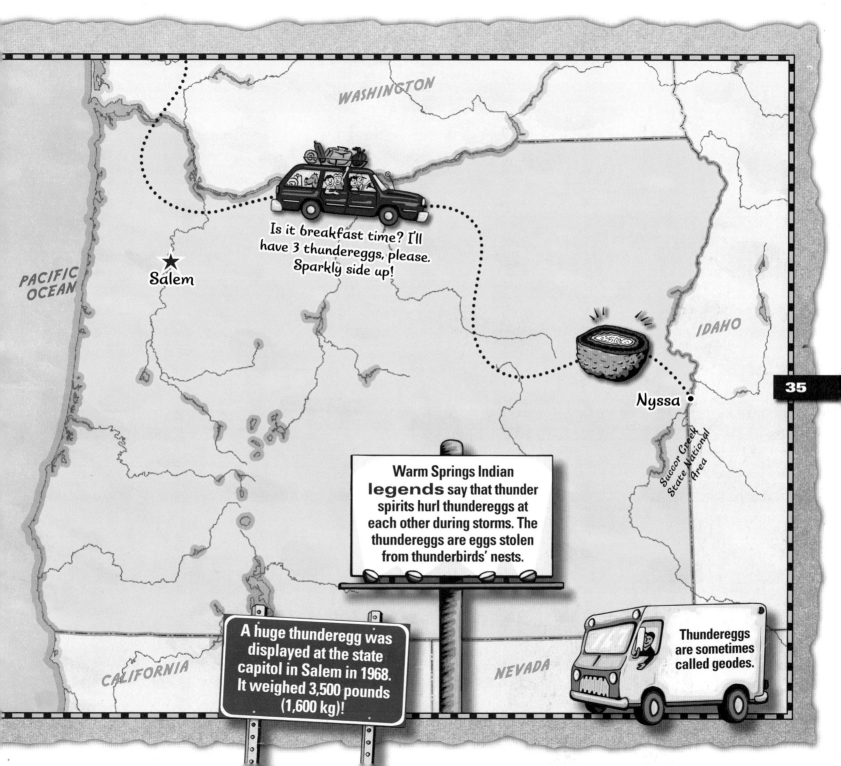

WASHINGTON

PACIFIC OCEAN

★ Salem

Is it breakfast time? I'll have 3 thundereggs, please. Sparkly side up!

IDAHO

Nyssa

35

Succor Creek State National Area

Warm Springs Indian **legends** say that thunder spirits hurl thundereggs at each other during storms. The thundereggs are eggs stolen from thunderbirds' nests.

A huge thunderegg was displayed at the state capitol in Salem in 1968. It weighed 3,500 pounds (1,600 kg)!

CALIFORNIA

NEVADA

Thundereggs are sometimes called geodes.

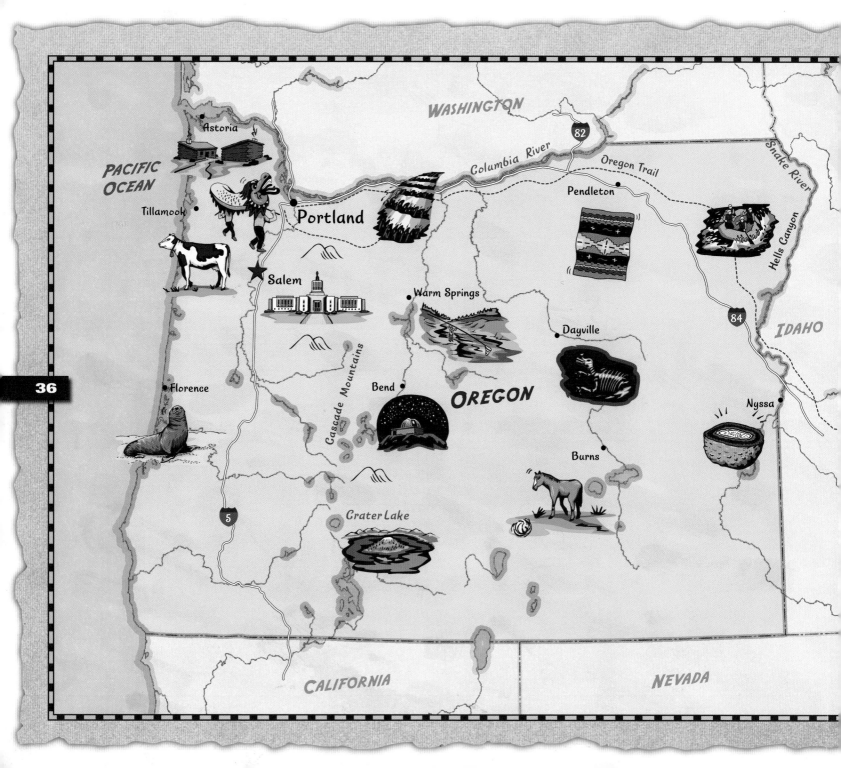

OUR TRIP

We visited many amazing places on our trip! We also met a lot of interesting people along the way. Look at the map on the left. Use your finger to trace all the places we have been.

What is the country's deepest river gorge? See page 8 for the answer.

Where was cartoonist Matt Groening born? Page 9 has the answer.

Where is the All-Indian Rodeo held? See page 13 for the answer.

How long did a trip across the Oregon Trail take? Look on page 18 for the answer.

Where did the Oregon Trail begin? Page 19 has the answer.

What is the origin of the word *Salem*? Turn to page 20 for the answer.

How long does Portland's Chinese New Year celebration last? Look on page 22 for the answer.

How many cows live in Tillamook? Turn to page 31 for the answer.

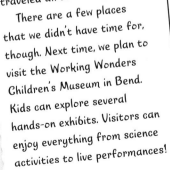

That was a great trip! We have traveled all over Oregon!
There are a few places that we didn't have time for, though. Next time, we plan to visit the Working Wonders Children's Museum in Bend. Kids can explore several hands-on exhibits. Visitors can enjoy everything from science activities to live performances!

More Places to Visit in Oregon

WORDS TO KNOW

ancestors (AN-sess-turz) parents, grandparents, great-grandparents, and so on

bulbs (BUHLBZ) underground buds from which some plants grow

corrals (kor-ALZ) fenced pens where horses are kept

curds (KURDZ) lumps formed when milk is thickened by heating or age

elders (ELL-durz) older people respected for being wise

fossils (FOSS-uhlz) prints or remains of plants or animals found in rock

Hispanic (hiss-PAN-ik) having roots in Spanish-speaking lands

immigrants (IM-uh-gruhnts) people who move from their homeland to another country

legends (LEJ-undz) imaginary tales handed down from earlier times

observatory (uhb-ZUR-vuh-tor-ee) a building set up for watching stars and distant objects

pioneers (pie-uh-NEERZ) the 1st people to explore or settle in an unknown land

plankhouse (PLANK-howss) a long log house built by certain northwestern Indian peoples

reservation (rez-ur-VAY-shuhn) a piece of land set aside for special use, such as for Native Americans

ruts (RUHTS) deep grooves or ditches

traditional (truh-DISH-uh-nuhl) following long-held customs

whey (HWAY) the watery part of milk that separates from the curds

Oregon covers 95,997 square miles (248,631 sq km). It's the 10th-largest state in size.

STATE SYMBOLS

State animal: American beaver

State beverage: Milk

State bird: Western meadowlark

State dance: Square dance

State fish: Chinook salmon

State flower: Oregon grape

State gemstone: Oregon sunstone

State insect: Oregon swallowtail butterfly

State mushroom: Pacific golden chanterelle

State nut: Hazelnut

State rock: Thunderegg (geode)

State seashell: Oregon hairy triton (conch)

State tree: Douglas fir

State flag

State seal

STATE SONG

"Oregon, My Oregon"

Words by J. A. Buchanan, music by Henry B. Murtagh

Land of the Empire Builders, Land of the Golden West;
Conquered and held by free men, Fairest and the best.
Onward and upward ever, Forward and on, and on;
Hail to thee, Land of Heroes, My Oregon.

Land of the rose and sunshine, Land of the summer's breeze;
Laden with health and vigor, Fresh from the Western seas.
Blest by the blood of martyrs, Land of the setting sun;

Hail to thee, Land of Promise, My Oregon.

**Can you find the Needles around Haystack Rock?
They're the smaller rocks.**

FAMOUS PEOPLE

Beard, James (1903-1985), chef and author

Carver, Raymond (1938-1988), author

Cleary, Beverly (1916-), children's book author

Duniway, Abigail Jane Scott (1834-1915), leader of the women's rights movement

Groening, Matt (1954-), cartoonist and creator of *The Simpsons*

Hatfield, Mark (1922-), politician

Joseph, Chief (ca. 1840-1904), American Indian leader

Kingman, Dave (1948-), baseball player

Le Guin, Ursula K. (1929-), author

Markham, Edwin (1852-1940), poet

McGinley, Phyllis (1905-1978), poet and author

McLoughlin, John (1784-1857), fur trader who helped settle Oregon

Miller, Joaquin (1837-1913), poet

Pauling, Linus (1901-1994), chemist and Nobel Prize winner

Powell, Jane (1929-), actor and singer

Prefontaine, Steve (1951-1975), runner

Rashad, Ahmad (1949-), football player and sportscaster

Reed, John (1887-1920), journalist

Schroeder, Patricia (1940-), politician

Simon, Norton (1907-1993), industrialist and art collector

TO FIND OUT MORE

At the Library
Cleary, Beverly. *A Girl from Yamhill: A Memoir.* New York: Morrow, 1988.

Hermes, Patricia. *The Wild Year.* New York: Scholastic, 2003.

Klingel, Cynthia, and Robert B. Noyed. *Chief Joseph: Chief of the Nez Percé.* Chanhassen, Minn.: The Child's World, 2003.

Simms, Laura, and Michael McCurdy. *The Bone Man: A Native American Modoc Tale.* New York: Hyperion Books, 1997.

Smith, Marie, Roland Smith, and Michael Roydon (illustrator). *B Is for Beaver: An Oregon Alphabet.* Chelsea, Mich.: Sleeping Bear Press, 2003.

On the Web
Visit our home page for lots of links about Oregon:
http://www.childsworld.com/links

Note to Parents, Teachers, and Librarians: We routinely verify our Web links to make sure they are safe, active sites—so encourage your readers to check them out!

Places to Visit or Contact
Oregon Historical Society
1200 SW Park Avenue
Portland, OR 97205
503/222-1741
For more information about the history of Oregon

Oregon Tourism Commission
775 Summer Street, NE
Salem, OR 97301
800/547-7842
For more information about traveling in Oregon

INDEX

Bye, Beaver State. We had a great time. We'll come back soon!